# 📖 READERS

## Level 2

## Level 3

# A Note to Parents

DK READERS is a compelling program for beginning readers, designed in conjunction with leading literacy experts, including Dr. Linda Gambrell, Professor of Education at Clemson University. Dr. Gambrell has served as President of the National Reading Conference, the College Reading Association, and the International Reading Association.

Beautiful illustrations and superb full-color photographs combine with engaging, easy-to-read stories and informational texts to offer a fresh approach to each subject in the series. Each DK READER is guaranteed to capture a child's interest while developing his or her reading skills, general knowledge, and love of reading.

The five levels of DK READERS are aimed at different reading abilities, enabling you to choose the books that are exactly right for your child:

**Pre-level 1:** Learning to read
**Level 1:** Beginning to read
**Level 2:** Beginning to read alone
**Level 3:** Reading alone
**Level 4:** Proficient readers

The "normal" age at which a child begins to read can be anywhere from three to eight years old. Adult participation through the lower levels is very helpful for providing encouragement, discussing storylines, and sounding out unfamiliar words.

No matter which level you select, you can be sure that you are helping your child learn to read, then read to learn!

LONDON, NEW YORK,
MELBOURNE, MUNICH, AND DELHI

**For DK/BradyGames**
**Publisher** David Waybright
**Editor-in-Chief** H. Leigh Davis
**Licensing Director** Mike Degler
**International Translations**
Brian Saliba
**Title Manager** Tim Fitzpatrick

**For DK Publishing**
**Publishing Director** Beth Sutinis
**Licensing Editor** Nancy Ellwood

**Reading Consultant**
Linda B. Gambrell, Ph.D.

Produced by
**Shoreline Publishing Group LLC**
**President** James Buckley Jr.
**Designer** Tom Carling, carlingdesign.com

DK/BradyGAMES
800 East 96th St., 3rd floor
Indianapolis, IN 46240

09 10 11 10 9 8 7 6 5 4

A catalog record for this book is available from the Library of Congress.

ISBN: 978-0-7566-4434-5 (Paperback)
ISBN: 978-0-7566-4477-2 (Hardback)

Printed and bound by Lake Book

Discover more at
# www.dk.com

**DK** READERS

BEGINNING TO READ ALONE **2**

# Meet the
# Pokémon

Written by Michael Teitelbaum

DK Publishing

*Empoloeon, Torterra, and Infernape.*

Welcome to the amazing world
of Pokémon [POH-kee-mohn]!
Pokémon come in many shapes
and sizes. Each one has its own
personality. They can be friendly or

tough, quiet or loud. They live in many places, such as cities or wild places.

Pokémon can be very smart. They can be led and taught by a good Pokémon Trainer.

Pokémon are good at battling each other. Different Pokémon have different abilities. They use these abilities to win their battles.

There are many different types of Pokémon. If you know the type of a Pokémon, you know where it likes to live. You will know its strengths or weaknesses. This can help you know how a Pokémon will do in battle.

*Monferno is Fire-type. Grotle is Grass-type.*

For example, in a battle, a Water-type Pokémon would probably beat a Fire-type Pokémon. A Fire-type Pokémon would likely beat a Grass-type.

*Raichu is an Electric-type Pokémon.*

There are 17 Pokémon types. Some of the other Pokémon types are Rock, Electric, Bug and Flying. Other types are Water and Normal.

*Prinplup is a Water-type.*

Pokémon evolve. That means that they change. When this happens, it's called an evolution. Take Chimchar for example.

*Monferno*

Chimchar is the first step in this evolution. It's a smaller Pokémon, very friendly—and hot! Later, Chimchar evolves into Monferno. It looks different and is more powerful.

*Chimchar*

Monferno is also bigger.
It evolves into Infernape.
Look how big it has become!
That's one powerful Pokémon!

Infernape looks very different from
Chimchar . . . but that's
how Pokémon evolve.
Pokémon can evolve
when they are
happy. They
also evolve
when they
become more
skilled in
battle.

*Infernape*

*This is a map showing the Sinnoh Region.*

Pokémon and their Trainers
live, play, train, battle, and have
adventures in lots of places.

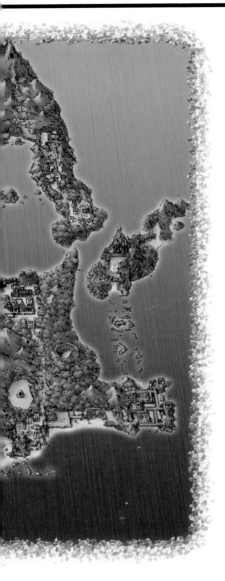

The Pokémon world is divided into many regions. These include the Kanto [KAN-toe] Region, the Johto [JOE-toe] Region, the Sinnoh [SIN-oh] Region, the Hoenn [HOH-en] Region, and the Orange Islands.

Each region is made up of many cities. Pokémon can be found in every city in every region.

Trainers are people that catch and train Pokémon. They can be kind to their Pokémon. Pokémon and their trainers quickly become friends.

The trainer takes the Pokémon

to a gym. There, the Pokémon learns how to battle other Pokémon.

To catch a Pokémon, trainers need a Poké Ball. Trainers throw their Poké Balls to catch Pokémon.  They carry their Pokémon around in Poké Balls. How do giant Pokémon fit into a tiny ball? That's just how it goes in the Pokémon world!

## Pokémon Gyms

Trainers train their Pokémon in gyms. Many cities have their own gyms. Each gym has a Gym Leader.

*Fuchsia City Gym*

Ash Ketchum is a Pokémon Trainer. He wants to become the world's greatest Pokémon Master. Ash is from Pallet Town in the Kanto Region. Pikachu is Ash's faithful friend and the first Pokémon Ash ever got. Ash got Pikachu from his friend Professor Oak.

Nobody knows more about Pokémon than Professor Oak. He gives many new trainers their first Pokémon. He also gives them their Poké Balls. Professor Oak collects information about Pokémon. He puts all this information into the Pokédex.

*Ash Ketchum
and Pikachu.*

15

*Pokémon Trainer
Dawn and her
Poké Ball.*

Ash's friend Dawn is from Twinleaf Town in the Sinnoh Region. She got her Pokémon from Professor Rowan, another famous Pokémon teacher. Her first Pokémon was a Piplup.

Misty is another one of Ash's best friends. She is also the Gym Leader of the Cerulean City Gym. Misty loves training Water-type Pokémon.

Ash's friend Brock is an older and more experienced Pokémon Trainer. Brock is the Pewter City Gym Leader. His favorite Pokémon are Rock-type Pokémon.

Pikachu was the first Pokémon that
Ash was given. Ash and Pikachu
quickly became great friends.
Pikachu can be moody and shy.
But it can also be cute and funny.
Pikachu doesn't like to be inside
a Poké Ball.

Pikachu can zap an opponent
with an Electric-type attack. It
stores electricity in its
cheeks. This comes

### Pikachu's Evolution
Pikachu can evolve from Pi-
chu. When Pikachu evolves, it
becomes Raichu. Raichu is its
final form.

*Pikachu often uses Electric-type attacks.*

in very handy when Pikachu is
battling another Pokémon. Pikachu
uses many types of attacks in these
battles. Some of the attack names
include Thundershock and Iron
Tail.

Let's meet some other popular
Pokémon. Chimchar is a Fire-type
Pokémon. It is an excellent climber.
Chimchar can climb a steep cliff.
It lives on the top of a mountain.

The fire on Chimchar's tail gets fuel
from its stomach! The fire
goes out when
Chimchar
sleeps.

*Chimchar*

Gible is a
Dragon-
and-
Ground-

*Gible*

type Pokémon. It nests in small holes in cave walls—it jumps out in surprise attacks! It evolves into Gabite. The scales of a Gabite can cure sickness. Gabite evolves into Garchomp. Garchomp can fly as fast as a jet.

Piplup is a Water-type Pokémon.
It is covered in down feathers. This
helps protect it from the cold. Piplup
evolves into Prinplup. Prinplup
lives alone, away
from all other
Pokémon. Prinplup
evolves into
Empoleon.
Empoleon has
three big horns and
is very powerful.

*Piplup*

Snorunt is an Ice-type Pokémon. It
lives in snowy areas. Some people
believe it brings good luck.

*Glalie*

Snorunt evolves into Glalie. Glalie protects itself by freezing water from the air to form ice armor.

Glalie then evolves into Froslass. Froslass freezes its enemies by using its ice-cold, freezing breath.

*Froslass*

Turtwig is a Grass-type Pokémon. It is made from soil and lives near lakes. It is a starter Pokémon for the Sinnoh Region. Turtwig evolves into Grotle. Grotle has trees growing on its hard shell. Grotle evolves into Torterra. Sometimes small Pokémon build nests on its back.

Snover is a Grass-and-Ice-type Pokémon. It has had little contact with humans. Snover evolves only once. It evolves into

*Turtwig*

*Abomasnow*

Abomasnow. Abomasnow is also
a Grass-and-Ice-type Pokémon. It
whips up blizzards in mountains,
blanketing them in snow.

Team Rocket is always trying to steal other people's Pokémon. They work for a boss who is a Pokémon Gym Leader named Giovanni.

What they really want most is Ash's Pikachu. Team Rocket also wants any rare and valuable Pokémon it can get!

### Team Rocket Leaders

Jessie can be very bossy. She can also be mean. She will stop at nothing to get her hands on Ash's Pikachu. James usually thinks up Team Rocket's plans to steal Pokémon. And all of his plans fail!

Jessie and James lead Team
Rocket. They come up with dumb
ways to steal Pokémon. One time
they dug a hole to catch Pokémon.
They fell into the hole themselves!

*Weavile uses Dark-type and Ice-type attacks in battle.*

Pokémon
love to battle.
Sometimes
the battle is friendly,
like a sporting event or a game.
Other times a trainer's Pokémon
will battle a wild Pokémon. If the
trainer's Pokémon wins, the wild
Pokémon then belongs to the
trainer.

But training Pokémon is not all about fighting. It's about friendship and caring for the Pokémon you collect. It's about respecting and enjoying each one's abilities and personality. Mostly, it's about fun.

*The chief Empoleon has the largest horns!*

So now you know a lot about Pokémon. You know that Pokémon come in all shapes, sizes, and types. You know that some live in oceans. Some live in caves. Some live in tall grass. Some even live on snowy mountains.

*Piplup, Chimchar, and Turtwig are ready for action!*

You know
that trainers
catch and then
train Pokémon.
You know that
Pokémon battle
and evolve. And *Pikachu*
you know that you always have
to watch out for Giovanni, Jessie,
James, and Team Rocket!

So what are you waiting for? It's time
to start your own Pokémon journey.

Who knows, maybe you will become
the next great Pokémon Trainer!

# Other Pokémon Evolutions

Abra evolves into Kadabra and then into Alakazam.

Squirtle evolves into Wartortle and then into Blastoise.

Chikorita evolves into Bayleef and then into Meganium.

Azurill evolves into Marill and then into Azumarill.

Whismur evolves into Loudred and then into Exploud.

*Abra*

*Kadabra*

*Alakazam*

# Index

**DK READERS**

My name is

I have read this book

Date